UNDERSTAND ACCOUNTING

Without Falling Asleep

A Simple Explanation of the Basics
for Non-accountants

by
Tim Shortridge

Understand Accounting
Without Falling Asleep:
A Simple Explanation of the Basics
for Non-accountants

Copyright © 2015 Tim Shortridge

All rights reserved. This includes the right to reproduce any portion of this book in any form without prior written permission of the author.

*For our daughter, Melanie, and our son, Richard...
We love you both past anything.*

Also by
Tim Shortridge:

Don't Cook Fish in the Company Microwave

No Place To Run

Out of Plumb

Sealing Fate

Table of Contents

FORWARD: Accounting Shouldn't Be So Hard...........vii
THE PURPOSE OF ACCOUNTING 1
   Three Parts of a Financial Transaction........................3
   What is an Accounting System?....................................4
BASIC FINANCIAL STATEMENTS 7
CREATING A BALANCE SHEET 9
   Assets 10
   Liabilities...11
   Equity 12
ENTERING FINANCIAL TRANSACTIONS
   1 – Open a Checking Account....................................15
   2 – Borrow Money from a Bank 17
   3 – Buy a Desk and Computer 19
   4 – Buy Inventory Net 30 20
   5 – Sell Inventory Net 30 22
   5-Part 2 – Change in Inventory 24
   6 – Pay Rent 26
CLOSING THE BALANCE SHEET...............................28
CREATING A PROFIT & LOSS STATEMENT..........32
DEBITS & CREDITS - DEFINED 39
   On the Balance Sheet 40
   On the Profit and Loss Statement..............................41
ACCRUAL VS. CASH 43
2 OUT OF 3 AIN'T BAD..46

FORWARD

Accounting Shouldn't Be So Hard

The subject of accounting can strike fear into the hearts of many people, but it shouldn't. Accounting is not rocket science. It's really just *counting*, but with a stammer. It's what I do for a living – Ac-counting. I *count* things.

Accounting isn't even mathematics. It's arithmetic. What do accountants do? We add. We subtract. We multiply. We divide. When we want to get really tricky, we do percentages.

If accounting is really that simple, you might be wondering why accounting classes are so hard. You probably already know the answer. It's because they tend to be so mind-numbingly boring. And why is that? It might be because they are taught by accountants.

I am *not* saying that it's a prerequisite to receiving your bachelor's degree in accounting that you have your personality surgically removed. However, it does appear that it might be a requirement for teaching accounting classes.

You are probably not aware of this, but *Accounting* is to professions, what *Denny's* is to restaurants. You see, no one ever goes to Denny's, you just kind of end up there because nothing else is open. It's the same for the accounting profession. No one sets out in life to be an accountant.

If you were to interview 10,000 eighth graders and ask them, "What do you want to be when you grow up?" Imagine how many would answer with, "I want to be an accountant." None. That's because no one sets out in life to be an accountant. You just kind of end up there.

Accounting was my sixth major in college.

I graduated from high school in 1970 (yes, I am that old, don't rub it in), and I set off for the University of Maryland with the declared major of civil engineering. I didn't know what civil engineering was, but I thought it sounded cool. My real major was partying.

I dropped out after my freshman year and enlisted in the Air Force to avoid getting drafted. My dad had spent two tours of duty in Vietnam, and I wasn't interested in following in his footsteps.

While I was still in the Air Force, I returned to college in the evenings as a Psychology major. The Psychology classes I took didn't make sense to me, and I only lasted for a semester before dropping out again.

After the Air Force, I got married and had two children. Our finances were *not* good, and we struggled to make ends meet.

I decided to return to college because the GI Bill would send me a monthly check that would be greater than my college expenses. I could actually make a little extra money by going back to school. So, I did.

This time, however, I majored in something I thought I could use to make money, Real Estate.

I received an Associate's degree in Real Estate in 1981 and quickly discovered that it wasn't the wellspring of financial success that I thought it would be. Since I had more time left on my GI Bill, I returned to college in 1982 with a Computer Programming major.

After one semester taking both COBOL and FORTRAN classes, I knew computer programming wasn't for me. So, I switched my major to Business Administration and earned my second Associate's degree the following year.

It was while I was working toward my Associate's degree in Business Administration that I was introduced to accounting. It was love at first study. Despite the lack of enthusiasm from my instructors, the subject made perfect sense to me. Unlike any other major I had tried, in accounting the numbers either added up or they didn't. Plus, accounting helped me to better understand business, and I was convinced that business would be our path to financial stability.

So, I changed my major to Accounting and received my Bachelor's degree in 1985. I feel very fortunate to have ended up in the accounting profession, and it has been (as they say on Saturday Night Live) very, very good to me.

I left corporate America in 1992 and started my own business setting up accounting systems for small businesses and teaching the non-accountant owners how to use them. Over the years, through trial and error, I developed this simple explanation of the basics of accounting.

I hope you find it as helpful as my clients have.

A Quick Note on Learning

In his book, *The 7 Habits of Highly Effective People*, Stephen R. Covey describes a way to significantly improve a person's understanding of anything they study. Rather than study for the purpose of learning, you should study for the purpose of teaching someone else.

By studying with the intention of teaching someone else, you change how you view the material you are studying, and that paradigm shift greatly improves your ability to understand.

I have found this technique quite effective, and I recommend you do the following:
1. Think of someone you know who could benefit from a better understanding of basic accounting.
2. Contact them right now, before you proceed, and set up a time to meet within the next 48 hours.
3. While you study this book, take notes on how *you* will teach it.
4. Keep your appointment and teach them these basics.

If you do this, both of you will benefit.

THE PURPOSE OF ACCOUNTING

The purpose of accounting is to accurately reflect the financial activity of an organization. There are three key parts to this statement that need further discussion:

Accurately. Accurately does *not* mean perfect down to the penny. That is an unrealistic expectation. We do expect accounting reports to be *reasonably* accurate. Reasonably accurate means someone can look at the accounting reports and understand the big picture of how the company is doing. It doesn't matter if a report says a company has $25,137.45 in cash when it actually has $25,215.15. That $77.70 difference doesn't change anyone's opinion about how the company is doing overall. However, if a report says a company has $137.45 in cash when it actually has $25,137.45 that could change how someone thinks the company is doing. It would depend on the size of the company. Even an extra $25,000 wouldn't change the big picture for a company like General Motors, but it could make a huge difference to a small restaurant wondering if they had enough money to cover payroll.

In accounting, when we say accurate, we mean reasonably accurate.

Accounting reports are of no use to anyone if they are not reasonably accurate. I frequently get asked by my clients, "Do the financial reports look good?" I explain that financial reports look neither good nor bad. They are either *accurate* or *inaccurate*. Accurate reports can tell you whether a company is performing well or poorly. But inaccurate reports can't. In fact, inaccurate reports *misrepresent* how a company is doing. And that can lead to bad business decisions.

Reflect. Accounting reports are meant to reflect what is actually happening in a business, not what someone wishes was happening in a business. I once worked for a Chief Financial Officer who thought he could dramatically improve the company's performance by making major changes to the financial statements so they would look better. What nonsense.

A company's performance is a company's performance. Changing the financial statements to look better doesn't change what has already happened. It only makes the financial statements inaccurate. That CFO happened to be one of the reasons I left Corporate America.

Financial Activity. Financial activity is the movement of money. In accounting, the term *movement of money* can mean cash moving now or it can mean the promise of cash moving later. If a business owner writes a check to a vendor to purchase inventory, that movement of money would be cash moving now. If the vendor doesn't require payment for 30 days, it would be the promise of cash moving later (the business owner has promised to pay the vendor within 30 days).

The movement of money is what accountants count. However, accountants don't refer to it as the *movement of money*, we just refer to it as *money*.

If a business activity doesn't involve money, accountants don't count it. When a business owner decides on a name for her business, that is a business activity. But her accountant won't count it until there is money involved, whether she pays now or promises to pay later.

To put it another way, the purpose of accounting is to keep track of the movement of money into and out of a business by counting it with reasonable accuracy.

Keep in mind, business happens in the real world. With real people working with other real people in real places and doing things that help other real people. Business does not happen in the accounting system of a company. That accounting system is only there to report what has already happened in the real world.

Remember, accounting deals with the past. Accountants count things that have *already* happened. Changing a report just to make it look a certain way doesn't change what actually happened. It only changes the report.

Think of accounting as a mirror for a company. You want that mirror to reflect a clean, reasonably accurate image of the company's financial activity, not a funhouse distortion.

How do accountants achieve this purpose? We count.

What do we count? Financial activity.

How do we count financial activity? One transaction at a time.

It doesn't matter if an accountant works for a small restaurant on a corner in downtown Boise, or she works for General Motors in Detroit, she still counts financial transactions. And she counts them one at a time. General Motors just has a lot more financial transactions. Which is why they employ an army of accountants to count them all.

In order to properly count a financial transaction, an accountant must understand it. To understand a financial transaction, she needs to understand each of its three parts.

Three Parts of a Financial Transaction

1. Money comes **_FROM_** someplace.
2. It goes **_TO_** someplace.
3. And it does so for a **_REASON_**.

Let's look at an example of a financial transaction. An entrepreneur decides to start a business. She goes to the bank and opens a business checking account by writing a personal

check for a hundred dollars. That would be a financial transaction. What would be the three parts of it?
1. Where did the money come *from*? Her personal checking account.
2. Where did the money go *to*? The business checking account.
3. ***Why***? To open the business checking account.

Knowing all three parts means you understand this financial transaction, and understanding it enables you to count it accurately.

If you see a deposit on the checking account statement of a business, then you know at least one part of the financial transaction. You know where the money went (into the checking account). But you also need to know where the money come from and why in order to count it accurately.

If the money came from a customer who was buying a product from the company, it would be counted differently than if the money came from an owner who was investing in the company.

In accounting, we count each financial transaction by entering it into an accounting system. We do this one transaction at a time, and our entry is based on all three parts of each transaction.

What is an Accounting System?

An accounting system is everything a business uses to accurately collect, count, track, and maintain information on financial transactions. Many people think of an accounting *program* as an accounting system. An accounting program is only one part of an overall accounting system. It's a tool an accountant uses, but it's only one of the tools.

How does an accountant know that a financial transaction has occurred? Information must flow into the accounting department. That information could be coming from sales people out on the road who are hand-writing invoices and mailing copies to accounting, or it could be downloaded electronically from the company's website. Vendors might

Understand Accounting

mail bills to accounting to be paid later by check, or electronic information could be downloaded from the bank showing any automatic withdrawals made by vendors. All of the data collection processes that are used are part of the overall accounting system.

One of the most familiar parts of an accounting system are the records accountants maintain to keep track of all the numbers they collect. Back in the old days of manual accounting using paper and pencils, these records were called a company's *Book of Accounts*. That name has since been shortened to just *Books* (e.g., keeping the books, or juggling the books, or cooking the books). Few companies keep their books manually, anymore. Computer programs are far more efficient, more accurate, and less expensive.

One of the most critical parts of an accounting system is document storage. Evidence of a financial transaction is called a source document. It could be a bank deposit slip. It could be a vendor bill. It could be many things. Accounting departments receive lots of different types of source documents, and all these source documents must be stored in such a way that they can be found later. The company's filing system is also part of its overall accounting system.

In 1975, I was the loan officer for a federal credit union in Riverside, California. The National Credit Union Administration (NCUA) arrived in November to audit our books. The NCUA is the government entity that insures deposits in a federal credit union much the same way as the FDIC insures deposits in federal banks.

The auditor was looking through our records and pulled out one of our auto loans. He handed it to me and said, "You should have a pink slip for the car that is collateral on this loan. You have ninety seconds to give it to me."

I looked at him in surprise. "Ninety seconds?"

He said, "If it takes longer than ninety seconds to find a document, you need to improve your filing system."

I've never forgotten this lesson. How many companies could find a source document in ninety seconds? By the way,

I handed the pink slip to the auditor in less than sixty seconds. I guess I was destined to be an accountant.

My point is, an accounting system includes everything needed to collect, count, track, and maintain all the information about the financial transactions of a business.

Four Essential Questions Every Accounting System Must Answer

Every accounting system must provide management with answers to *at least* these four essential questions:

1. ***Who owes the company money?*** If a company doesn't know who owes it money, then it won't collect as much as it should, and this can be hard on its cash flow.

2. ***Who does the company owe money to?*** Paying bills on time is essential to maintaining good relationships with vendors. And if a company wants to keep its employees happy, it had better pay them on time as well.

3. ***How much money does the company have?*** When paying those bills and paychecks, it is best if the checks don't bounce.

4. ***Is the company making any money?*** Without knowing if they are making money, management can't fix what is not working or do more of what is working.

Sadly, there are thousands of business owners who cannot get their accounting systems to answer these four essential questions. Sadder still, most of them will be out of business within the next two years.

A good accounting system can answer these four essential questions. A good accounting system can answer a lot more questions than just these four questions, but these are the *most* important.

BASIC FINANCIAL STATEMENTS

Accountants use two basic financial statements to accurately reflect the financial activity of a business. These financial statements provide an overview of what is happening inside the company.

Balance Sheet

The Balance Sheet is a *snapshot* of the financial position of a company. It's a snapshot because the report is as of one moment in time, for example it could be as of midnight on December 31st.

On New Year's Eve, after everyone else has left the business to go celebrate, the accountants sneak into the building and start counting. They count how much money is in the checking account. They count how much money customers owe the company. They count how much inventory is in the warehouse and what it cost. They count how much money the business owes to its vendors.

All night long, the accountants are counting, counting, counting. They are in ac-counting heaven.

By morning, they organize all the totals into a Balance Sheet. That Balance Sheet lists the value of everything the company owns and the value of all the money it owes to others. However, that Balance Sheet is only a snapshot. It is only accurate as of midnight on December 31st. It's only accurate as of that one moment in time because the first financial transaction of the New Year will change the numbers on the Balance Sheet.

Of course, accountants don't really count all night to prepare a Balance Sheet, but you get the idea.

Profit and Loss Statement

The Profit and Loss Statement (or P&L) is actually part of the Balance Sheet. It resides in the Equity section which I will explain in a minute. The P&L is the financial statement that answers the fourth essential question above: ***Is the company making any money?***

Unlike the Balance Sheet, the Profit and Loss Statement covers a *period of time*. Did the company make any money last year? Did the company make any money last quarter? Did the company make any money last month?

It does this by listing all the income and expenses for the company over that time period. When you subtract the total expenses for a company from the total income for the company, the difference is the Profit, assuming the company has more income than expenses. If the expenses are more than the income, then the company is said to have suffered a loss during that period.

Hence the name, *Profit* and *Loss* Statement.

CREATING A BALANCE SHEET

Let me step you through creating a balance sheet. Your participation will accomplish two things:
1. It will enhance your understanding of this material.
2. It will keep you awake (as promised in the title).

Please take out two blank sheets of paper at least 8.5 inches wide by 11 inches tall. With the first sheet of paper, you will create a Balance Sheet. You will use the other sheet of paper later. So set it aside for now.

At the top center of your paper, write **BALANCE SHEET**.

On the left side of the paper, and a little below the words **BALANCE SHEET**, write **ASSETS**.

On the right side of the paper, and aligned with the word **ASSETS**, write **LIABILITIES**.

Draw a horizontal line across the top of the page below the words **ASSETS** and **LIABILITIES**. Then draw a vertical line down the center of your paper from the horizontal line to the bottom of the page. The two lines should look like a *T*.

You should now have two blank columns on your paper, one under the word **ASSETS** and the other under the word **LIABILITIES** that look something like this:

BALANCE SHEET

ASSETS	LIABILITIES

Assets

Assets are things a company owns that have value.

For example, money has value. So, if a company has any money (hopefully it does), that money would be an asset. If the company has customers who owe the company money (called Accounts Receivable), the amount they owe would also be an asset of the company. If a company has purchased things it intends to sell to others (called Inventory), those things have value and are another asset. And if a company has purchased any furniture or equipment for their office, the furniture and equipment would also be assets.

There are lots of other types of assets, but I'm going to keep it simple for this exercise.

Down the left side of your sheet of paper, near the edge and below the word *ASSETS*, please write the following (leaving some room between the words):

Checking Account
Accounts Receivable
Inventory
Furniture & Equipment

These are the assets we are going to use during this exercise. Your paper should now look something like this:

BALANCE SHEET

ASSETS	LIABILITIES
Checking Account	
Accounts Receivable	
Inventory	
Furniture & Equipment	

Liabilities

Liabilities are money a company owes to others.

For example, if a company has purchased things from a vendor, but hasn't paid for them because the vendor doesn't require payment until later (called Accounts Payable), the amount owed is a liability. If a company uses a credit card to purchase office supplies, the amount owed on the credit card is a liability. And if a company borrows money from a bank, the amount owed to the bank is also a liability.

There are lots of other types of liabilities, but I'm going to keep these simple as well.

Down the center of your sheet of paper, to the right of the center line and below the word ***LIABILITIES***, write the following (and leave room between these words also):

Accounts Payable
Credit Card
Bank Loan

These are the Liabilities we are going to use during this exercise. Your paper should now look something like this:

BALANCE SHEET

ASSETS	LIABILITIES
Checking Account	Accounts Payable
Accounts Receivable	Credit Card
Inventory	Bank Loan
Furniture & Equipment	

Equity

Equity is one of the trickier accounting concepts, and is best understood with a Real Estate example. If you own a home, it has a value. Let's say you could sell it for $250,000. However, you probably borrowed money from a bank or mortgage company in order to buy it. Let's say you owe $200,000 on your home.

The *equity* you have in your home is the difference between what your home is worth and what you owe on it. In this case, you would have $50,000 in equity. You could also think of equity as what you would have left over if you sold your home and paid off your mortgage.

The equity of a business is similar to the equity in a home. The value of all the assets of the business minus the total of all the liabilities is the equity. If a business sold all their assets and paid off all their liabilities, the cash they would have left over would be their equity.

For a successful business owner, the equity in their business will eventually exceed any equity they might have in their real estate. Think Bill Gates, Steve Jobs, or Mark Zuckerberg.

Although the total equity of any company is always the difference between the value of its Assets and the total of its Liabilities, different types of companies have different types of equity within that total. A sole proprietorship classifies its equity differently than a partnership, corporation, or Limited Liability Company (LLC).

I'm going to use the equity classifications of a sole proprietorship for the purpose of this exercise.

Equity can be increased in a company in different ways. For example, an owner could put money into the company (called an Owner Contribution). Or the company can make a profit. Profits increase the equity of a company. Equity can also be reduced in different ways. If an owner takes money out of a company (called Owner Draw), the equity goes

Understand Accounting 13

down. Or if the company experiences a period of losses, those losses reduce the company's equity.

In the center of the right-hand column of your paper, just below the word ***Bank Loan***, please write ***Equity***. Then draw a horizontal line from the vertical center line to the right edge of your paper just below the word ***Equity***.

Down the center of your sheet of paper, just to the right of the center line and below the word ***Equity***, please write the following (and leave room between these words also):

Owner Contributions – Add
Owner Draws – (Subtract)
Profits or (Losses)

Leave at least three inches below the words ***Profits or (Losses)*** and the bottom of the page. We'll be adding more classifications there before we're through.

These are the Equity classifications for a sole proprietor that we are going to use during this exercise.

You should now have a blank Balance Sheet on your paper that looks something like this:

BALANCE SHEET

ASSETS	LIABILITIES
Checking Account	Accounts Payable
Accounts Receivable	Credit Card
Inventory	Bank Loan
Furniture & Equipment	
	EQUITY
	Owner Contribution – Add
	Owner Draws – (Subtract)
	Profits or (Losses)

This balance sheet has classifications, but no amounts. Every business that has ever existed has started with this exact Balance Sheet. Before a business does anything financially, it has no Assets, no Liabilities, and no Equity.

In Accounting, we call each one of these classifications *accounts*. For example, we refer to the **Accounts Receivable** *account*, or the **Owner Contribution** *account*. Don't confuse this use of the word *account* with how banks use the word. Think of these accounts as buckets into which we will be putting numbers. We use these buckets to store numbers until we're ready to add them up and put the total on a report.

Your paper will be the books for our sample company. On it, you've listed all the asset accounts, all the liability accounts, and all the equity accounts. This is why the books used to be called the *book of accounts*.

We are now ready to enter some financial transactions into the books and see how those transactions change the Balance Sheet of our sample company.

ENTERING FINANCIAL TRANSACTIONS

Starting a business requires a business owner to make thousands of decisions. Does she want to provide services, or sell products, or do both? What services? What products? What name? What legal structure? Etc., etc., etc.

However, until the owner does something with money, her accountant doesn't have anything to count.

Transaction #1 – Open a Checking Account

For the purpose of this exercise, the first thing our owner will do with money is go to the bank and write a personal check for $100 to open a business checking account.

Remember, business happens in the real world. All we're trying to do as accountants is to accurately reflect this. So, what really happened? The owner got in her car and drove to the bank. She wrote a personal check for $100 and deposited it into the new business checking account. She returned from the bank with the deposit slip (our source document).

Do we understand this transaction? What are its three parts?
1. Where did the money come *from*? The owner's personal checking account.
2. Where did the money go *to*? The business checking account.
3. *Why*? To open the business checking account.

Good. Then let's enter this financial transaction into the blank Balance Sheet on your paper:
If the money came from the owner's personal checking account, then the owner is putting money into her business. We classify that as an Owner Contribution. The classification of Owner Contribution is in the Equity section of your Balance Sheet. Whenever a

business owner puts money into her business, she is increasing the equity of the company.

On your paper, in the equity section and below the words ***Owner Contribution – Add***, write +$100. Doing this records where the money came from.

Since the money went into the business checking account, below the words ***Checking Account*** in the assets section of your Balance Sheet, write +$100. This records where the money went and why.

Congratulations, you just entered your first financial transaction. You've taken a giant leap toward understanding accounting. Your balance sheet should now look like this:

BALANCE SHEET

ASSETS	LIABILITIES
Checking Account +$100	Accounts Payable
Accounts Receivable	Credit Card
Inventory	Bank Loan
Furniture & Equipment	
	EQUITY
	Owner Contribution – Add +$100
	Owner Draws – (Subtract)
	Profits or (Losses)

Please take a moment and notice that if you were to add up all the Assets of the company (the left-hand column), they would total $100. And if you were to add up all the Liabilities and Equity (the right-hand column), they would also total $100.

Hence the name, *Balance* Sheet.

Understand Accounting

If the total of the left-hand side of your Balance Sheet equals the total of the right-hand side, then your Balance Sheet is said to be *in balance*. If your Balance Sheet is in balance, then there is at least a chance that your financial statements are accurately reflecting the financial activity of the business.

However, if the total of the left-hand side of your Balance Sheet *does not* equal the total of the right-hand side, then your Balance Sheet is said to be *out of balance* and there is NO WAY your financial statements are accurately reflecting the financial activity of the business.

Just a little FYI…

Transaction #2 – Borrow Money from a Bank

The next day, our business owner goes down to her bank and, on bended knee, pleads with the banker to loan her some money to help her get her business going.

The banker, being the risk-taking entrepreneur that most bankers are, says, "Sure. I'll loan you $900 and you can pay it back over the next 36 months. We'll even deposit the money directly into the checking account you opened yesterday."

Not as much as she had hoped for, but she agrees and returns home with two more source documents, a loan agreement and another deposit slip.

What are the three parts of this transaction?
1. Where did the money come *from*? The bank loan.
2. Where did the money go *to*? The business checking account.
3. *Why*? To deposit the loan proceeds.

Let's enter this financial transaction into the Balance Sheet on your paper:
Since the money came from a bank loan, the owner owes this money to the bank. We classify this as a Liability, and use the Balance Sheet classification of

Bank Loan. Whenever a business owner borrows money, they are increasing the liabilities of their company.

On your paper, below the words **Bank Loan**, write +$900 to record where the money came from.

Since the money went into the business checking account, below the words **Checking Account** and next to the +$100 from transaction #1, write +$900. This records where the money went and why.

Congratulations, you have just entered your second financial transaction. Looking down both sides of your Balance Sheet, your total Assets should now equal $1,000, and so should the total of your Liabilities and Equity.

Is that what your balance sheet shows? Please check.

Go ahead. I'll wait.

Your balance sheet should look something like this:

BALANCE SHEET

ASSETS	LIABILITIES
Checking Account +$100 +$900	Accounts Payable
Accounts Receivable	Credit Card
Inventory	Bank Loan +$900
Furniture & Equipment	**EQUITY**
	Owner Contribution – Add +$100
	Owner Draws – (Subtract)
	Profits or (Losses)

Understand Accounting

Transaction #3 – Buy a Desk and Computer with a Credit Card

Our business owner is getting excited. She can clearly see her dream of owning her own business coming to life.

She jumps back in her car and drives to Staples where she buys a desk, a top-of-the-line computer, and a fully equipped printer/fax/scanner. Since she doesn't have enough money in her business checking account to pay the $3,500 they cost, she hands the cashier her credit card. This is one of her personal credit cards, but she has decided that she will use it exclusively for her business.

After stuffing all these purchases into her car, she drives home with her source document, the credit card receipt.

Once she's back home, she unpacks the boxes which are labeled, *Some assembly required.* And after four hours, her office is all set up in the downstairs spare room.

What are the three parts of this transaction?
1. Where did the money come *from*? Her credit card that she is planning to use exclusively for business.
2. Where did the money go *to*? Staples.
3. *Why*? To buy her desk, computer, and printer.

Let's enter this financial transaction into the Balance Sheet on your paper:

Since the money came from her "business" credit card, she owes this money to the credit card company. This would be another Liability, and the Balance Sheet classification would be Credit Card.

On your paper, below the words ***Credit Card***, write +$3,500 to record where the money came from.

Since the money went to buy her desk and computer, below the words ***Furniture & Equipment***, write +$3,500. This records where the money went and why.

Your balance sheet should now look something like this:

BALANCE SHEET

ASSETS	LIABILITIES
Checking Account +$100 +$900 Accounts Receivable Inventory Furniture & Equipment +$3,500	Accounts Payable Credit Card +$3,500 Bank Loan +$900 **EQUITY** Owner Contribution – Add +$100 Owner Draws – (Subtract) Profits or (Losses)

Transaction #4 – Buy Inventory with Terms of Net 30

After careful consideration, our business owner decides she will be in the business of selling stuff. She doesn't have any stuff to sell, but she knows a guy across town (a good friend, actually) who sells stuff.

She calls him on the phone and asks, "Will you sell me some of your stuff so I can sell it in my business?"

He says, "I've known you for years. Of course I will. Come over tomorrow. I'll sell you a carload of stuff for $1,200, and you don't have to pay me for 30 days."

The next day, she drives across town, loads up her car with boxes of stuff, and drives back home with another source document. This one is a vendor bill that isn't due for 30 days. This is called buying with terms of N*et 30*. *Net 30* means the bill isn't due for 30 days.

Understand Accounting

Once home, she unpacks her car and stacks the boxes of stuff along the wall of her dining room. After thinking about it, she decides to move the boxes into the garage.

What are the three parts of this transaction?
1. Where did the money come *from*? Her friend, the vendor. By not requiring payment right away, he effectively loaned her the money for 30 days.
2. Where did the money go *to*? Boxes of stuff.
3. *Why*? So she would have something to sell.

Let's enter this financial transaction into the Balance Sheet on your paper:
   Since the money came from her vendor, she owes this money to him. This would be another Liability, and the Balance Sheet classification would be Accounts Payable.
   On your paper, below the words *Accounts Payable*, write +$1,200 to record where the money came from.
   Since the money went to buy stuff for her to sell, below the asset classification of *Inventory*, write +$1,200. This records where the money went and why.

Let's take a quick look at your Balance Sheet. The total of all the Assets should now equal $5,700. And that should match the total of all the Liabilities and the Equity.

If both sides balance, then you're doing well. If they don't, please review your entries with the above instructions, find your mistake, and fix it.

By the way, everyone who does accounting makes mistakes. It's just part of the job. The key to being good at accounting is finding and fixing those mistakes before anyone else sees them.

All fixed? Back in balance? Excellent.

Your balance sheet should now look something like this:

BALANCE SHEET

ASSETS	LIABILITIES
Checking Account +$100 +$900 Accounts Receivable Inventory +$1,200 Furniture & Equipment +$3,500	Accounts Payable +$1,200 Credit Card +$3,500 Bank Loan +$900 **EQUITY** Owner Contribution – Add +$100 Owner Draws – (Subtract) Profits or (Losses)

Transaction #5 – Sell Inventory with Terms of Net 30

The next day, her neighbor walks by when her garage is open, and says, "I see you have some stuff stacked up in there. Would you be interested in selling any of it?"

She says, "Why yes, I happen to be in the business of selling stuff. And since you're my neighbor, and I know where you live, I will sell some of my stuff to you, and you don't have to pay me for 30 days."

The neighbor walks into her garage and looks through a few boxes. He selects a number of things to buy, and our owner tells him the total price for what he chose is $1,150.

He scratches his head, hems and haws, then agrees.

"Oops. I forgot the sales tax," she says. "That's another $92. So, your total comes to $1,242."

"Done," says the neighbor.

She gives him an invoice listing everything he bought, the price of each, the sales tax, and the terms of Net 30. He takes the invoice and the box of stuff he just bought, thanks her, and goes home.

Understand Accounting

She keeps a copy of the invoice (either printed or electronic) as her source document.

What are the three parts of this transaction?
1. Where did the money come *from*? This one is a little tricky. The money came from two different places. $1,150 came from the sale. This is the money she earned. The other $92 came from the sales tax, which is money she owes to the taxing authority.
2. Where did the money go *to*? A loan to the customer.
3. *Why*? So the customer could buy now and pay later.

Let's enter this financial transaction into the Balance Sheet on your paper:

Since some of the money came from the sale, we will need to list the Profit and Loss Statement accounts in the Equity section of the Balance Sheet. Under the words ***Profits or (Losses)***, please write ***Sales***.

This sale will increase the equity in the company, so to the right of the word ***Sales***, write +$1,150 to record where that money came from.

Once this sale is made and she has charged her customer sales tax, she owes that sales tax to the taxing authority. This would be another liability. Below the words ***Accounts Payable,*** and to the right of the +$1,200 from the last transaction, write +$92 to record where that money came from and why.

We also want to record that her customer now owes her money. In the Assets section of the Balance Sheet, below the words ***Accounts Receivable***, write +$1,242. Her customer owes her both the money for the sale and the money for the sales tax. This records where the money went.

Your balance sheet should now look something like this:

BALANCE SHEET

ASSETS	LIABILITIES
Checking Account +$100 +$900 Accounts Receivable +$1,242 Inventory +$1,200 Furniture & Equipment +$3,500	Accounts Payable +$1,200 +$92 Credit Card +$3,500 Bank Loan +$900
	EQUITY
	Owner Contribution – Add +$100 Owner Draws – (Subtract) Profits or (Losses) Sales +$1,150

Transaction #5 – Part 2, Change in Inventory

The sale of inventory is not just tricky because of sales tax, it is also tricky because there are two parts of the transaction. First is entering the sale, which we just did. Next, we need to record the change in inventory.

Does our owner still have $1,200 in inventory? Of course not. Her neighbor just took some of it home. So, we need to reduce her inventory by the cost of what she just sold to her neighbor. Let's say the cost was $550. She bought inventory for $550 and sold it for $1,150. Way to go!

Did she make $1,150 in profit on this sale? No, the stuff she sold cost her $550. So, we have to reduce her profit by the same amount as we reduced her inventory.

What are the three parts of this transaction?
1. Where did the money come *from*? Inventory.
2. Where did the money go *to*? To a reduction in her profit. We call this *Cost of Sales*.

Understand Accounting

3. *Why*? To record the reduction of her inventory that occurred when she sold some of it.

Let's enter this transaction into your Balance Sheet:

Since the money came from her inventory, below the word *Inventory*, and to the right of where you earlier wrote +$1,200, please write -$550. This will record where the money came from and why.

Since the money went to reducing her profit on the sale, we need to expand the Profit and Loss Statement in the Equity section of the Balance Sheet. Under the word *Sales*, please write *Cost of Sales*.

The cost of this sale will reduce the equity in the company, so to the right of the words *Cost of Sales*, write -$550 to record where the money went.

This sale is the trickiest transaction in this example. Is your Balance Sheet still in balance? Both sides should now total $6,392, and it should look something like this:

BALANCE SHEET

ASSETS	LIABILITIES
Checking Account +$100 +$900 Accounts Receivable +$1,242 Inventory +$1,200 -$550 Furniture & Equipment +$3,500	Accounts Payable +$1,200 +$92 Credit Card +$3,500 Bank Loan +$900
	EQUITY

	Owner Contribution – Add
	+$100
	Owner Draws – (Subtract)
	
	Profits or (Losses)
	  Sales +$1,150
	  Cost of Sales -$550

Transaction #6 – Pay Rent

Our business owner receives a notification from her Homeowners Association telling her that it is against the rules for her to run a business out of her house.

Rather than move, she decides to look through Craigslist for a small store front she could rent.

Within a few days, she finds one that she thinks might work and sets an appointment with the leasing agent so she can look at it. Once there, she is confident that it will work great.

She looks over the rental agreement, negotiates a lower price, and writes a check from her business checking account for $400 to pay the rent for the last two weeks of the month.

What are the three parts of this transaction?
1. Where did the money come *from*? The business checking account.
2. Where did the money go *to*? The landlord.
3. *Why*? To pay the rent.

Let's enter this financial transaction into the Balance Sheet on your paper:

- Since the money came from the business checking account, below the words **Checking Account**, to the right of where you earlier wrote +$900, please write -$400.
- Rent is an expense that reduces a company's overall profit. Since the money went to reducing her profit, we need to expand the Profit and Loss Statement in the Equity section of the Balance Sheet again. Under the words **Cost of Sales,** please write **Rent Expense**.
- The rent expense will reduce the equity in the company, so to the right of the words **Rent Expense**, write -$400 to record where the money went.

Your balance sheet should now look something like this:

BALANCE SHEET

ASSETS	LIABILITIES
Checking Account +$100 +$900 -$400 Accounts Receivable +$1,242 Inventory +$1,200 -$550 Furniture & Equipment +$3,500	Accounts Payable +$1,200 +$92 Credit Card +$3,500 Bank Loan +$900
	EQUITY

	Owner Contribution – Add
	+$100
	Owner Draws – (Subtract)
	
	Profits or (Losses)
	   Sales +$1,150
	   Cost of Sales -$550
	   Rent Expense -$400

You have entered each one of these transactions based on where the money came from, where it went to, and why. This is accounting. We're counting financial transactions one at a time. Some transactions are more complicated than others, but you can figure out how to count them properly by thinking about the flow of the money in the real world. Where did it come from? Where did it go to? Why?

Now, let's assume we are done with the accounting for this period and we're ready to close the balance sheet.

CLOSING THE BALANCE SHEET

The first thing we want to do is to enter totals for each account.

To the right of each Asset account, let's write the totals:
Checking Account total is $600
Accounts Receivable total is $1,242
Inventory total is $650
Furniture & Equipment total is $3,500

To ensure accuracy, all of these accounts should be reconciled. To reconcile an account means to compare what is in the balance sheet with something that is outside of the balance sheet.

We won't reconcile our sample accounts, but the accounts for a real company should be reconciled every month.

To reconcile the checking account, the transactions in the balance sheet should be compared to the transactions on the bank statement. Any differences should be researched and corrected as needed.

To reconcile Accounts Receivable, a list of the customers who owe the company money should be prepared, and the total of the list compared to the total on the balance sheet.

To reconcile Inventory, a list of inventory items and their costs from the accounting system should be compared with what is in the warehouse, plus what is in the trunk of the owner's car, plus tucked into nooks and crannies around the company, etc. Make any necessary corrections.

A list of all Furniture and Equipment that matches the balance sheet should be maintained and compared with what is still in the company. If something is gone, then the balance sheet should be adjusted. Why would something be gone? There are many possible reasons. Maybe the owner gave a company computer to her daughter who was heading off to college. Or maybe a display case broke when it was being

Understand Accounting

moved across the store, so it was hauled out to the trash. If something is on the balance sheet, but no longer in the company, then the balance sheet needs to be corrected.

At the bottom left of the assets section of the balance sheet, write *Total Assets*.

Then draw a line slightly above and to the right, aligned under the total for Furniture & Equipment. Below that line, write $5,992. This is the total of all the company's assets as of this one moment in time. If the sum of your totals doesn't match, please check your work for mistakes.

Draw two lines under the $5,992. In accounting, we use a double underline to mark a calculation for a column. In this case, the $5,992 is the sum of all the numbers above it.

Let's enter the totals to the right of each liability account:
Accounts Payable total is $1,292
Credit Card total is $3,500
Bank Loan total is $900

These accounts should also be reconciled.

For Accounts Payable, make a list of all the unpaid bills (which should be located in a file marked *Bills to be Paid*) and compare the total of that list with the balance sheet total.

Compare the credit card transactions in the balance sheet with those on the credit card statement.

And compare the bank loan balance with the balance on the loan statement.

At the bottom of the Liabilities section, write *Total Liabilities*. Then draw a line slightly above and to the right, aligned under the other totals. Below the line, write $5,692.

Draw a single line under $5,692. In accounting, we use a single underline to mark a subtotal in a column. This is the subtotal for all the company's liabilities.

Do the same thing for the Equity Section:
Owner Contributions total is $100
Owner Draws total is $0
Profits or (Losses) total is $200

It is not possible to reconcile the Equity accounts because we don't have anything to compare them to. Instead, they should be reviewed. If anything looks weird, it should be researched. For example, if you notice two month's rent is expensed in one month. That would be weird.

At the bottom of the Equity section write *Total Equity*, and draw a line to the right under the totals. Below the line write $300. This is the total of the company's Equity.

Draw another line under the $300. Below that line, write $5,992 and draw two lines under it. To the left, write *Total Liabilities & Equity*. Please note that it equals the total assets.

Your balance sheet should now look something like this:

BALANCE SHEET

ASSETS		LIABILITIES	
Checking Account +$100 +$900 -$400	$600	Accounts Payable +$1,200 +$92	$1,292
Accounts Receivable +$1,242	$1,242	Credit Card +$3,500	$3,500
Inventory +$1,200 -$550	$650	Bank Loan +$900	$900
Furniture & Equipment +$3,500	$3,500	**Total Liabilities**	$5,692

		EQUITY	
		Owner Contribution – Add +$100	$100
		Owner Draws – (Subtract)	$0

		Profits or (Losses)
		  Sales +$1,150
		  Cost of Sales -$550
		  Rent Expense -$400
			$200

		Total Equity	$300
Total Assets	$5,992	**Total Liabilities & Equity**	$5,992

Whew. We're still in balance.

Understand Accounting

This is how balance sheets are created. Each part of each financial transaction flows into the appropriate account classification. And then, as of one moment in time, we add up all of them to create a balance sheet.

Of course, we don't leave all the individual transaction numbers on the balance sheet. We also don't leave the Profit and Loss transactions on it, either. After we clear all those off and summarize the P&L, the balance sheet ends up looking more like this:

BALANCE SHEET

ASSETS		LIABILITIES	
Checking Account	$600	Accounts Payable	$1,292
Accounts Receivable	$1,242	Credit Card	$3,500
Inventory	$650	Bank Loan	$900
Furniture & Equipment	$3,500	**Total Liabilities**	$5,692
		EQUITY	
		Owner Contribution – Add	$100
		Owner Draws – (Subtract)	$0
		Profits or (Losses)	$200
		Total Equity	$300
Total Assets	$5,992	**Total Liabilities & Equity**	$5,992

This is an example of a side-by-side balance sheet. Most computer programs nowadays stack the assets on top of the liabilities and equity. It's a different format, but don't let that throw you. The fundamentals are exactly the same.

CREATING A
PROFIT & LOSS STATEMENT

Since we have summarized all of the sales, cost of sales, and expense transactions on the balance sheet into one number, we now want to provide detailed information on a separate Profit and Loss Statement (P&L).

Please take out your other blank sheet of paper and write across the top in the center *Profit and Loss Statement*. Then draw a line under it all the way from the left edge of the paper to the right edge of the paper.

Because we have all this room on this separate sheet of paper, we can break down the financial transaction information into more usable pieces for management. We do it like this:

    Near the edge of the left side of your paper and below the line, write ***Sales.***

    In the middle of the page, just below the line and aligned with the word ***Sales***, write ***Gizmo Sales.***

    Below the words ***Gizmo Sales*** write, ***Gadget Sales.***

    Under the words ***Gadget Sales***, but a little to the left (between the word ***Sales*** and the words ***Gadget Sales***), write ***Total Sales.***

Your P&L should look something like this:

PROFIT AND LOSS STATEMENT
___

Sales   Gizmo Sales
                             Gadget Sales
          Total Sales

The neighbor didn't just buy $1,150 worth of stuff. He actually bought $750 of Gizmos and $400 of Gadgets. Let's enter that sale into the P&L:

Just to the right of the words ***Gizmo Sales***, write $750.

Just to the right of the words *Gadget Sales* and below the $750 for Gizmo Sales, write 400 and draw a line under it (the dollar sign is not required because the number directly above has one).

All the way to the right, next to the edge of the paper, and aligned with the words *Total Sales*, write $1,150.

Your P&L should now look something like this:

PROFIT AND LOSS STATEMENT

Sales			
	Gizmo Sales	$750	
	Gadget Sales	400	
	Total Sales		$1,150

Breaking out the sales in this manner provides management with additional insight not available with reporting the total sales only. This level of detail is a more accurate reflection of the financial activity of this business.

Our business owner can now see that she is selling almost twice as many Gizmos as she is Gadgets. What she does with this information would vary depending on her business, industry, market conditions, and many other factors. At least she now has the information.

We want to break out the Cost of Sales in the same way:

On the left side of the paper, near the edge, directly below the word *Sales* and aligned horizontally just below the words *Total Sales*, write *Cost of Sales.*

In the middle of the page directly below the words *Gadget Sales* and aligned horizontally with the words *Cost of Sales*, write *Gizmo Costs.*

Below the words *Gizmo Costs* write, *Gadget Costs.*

Under the words *Gadget Costs*, but a little to the left (between the words *Cost of Sales* and the words *Gadget Costs*) and aligned directly under the words *Total Sales*, write *Total Cost of Sales.*

To the right of the words ***Gizmo Costs*** and below the $400 for Gadget Sales, write $350.

To the right of the words ***Gadget Costs*** and below the $350 for Gizmo Costs, write 200 and draw a line under it.

All the way to the right, and aligned with the words ***Total Cost of Sales*** and directly below the $1,150 for Total Sales, write $550 and draw a line under it.

Your P&L should now look something like this:

PROFIT AND LOSS STATEMENT

Sales		Gizmo Sales	$750	
		Gadget Sales	400	
	Total Sales			$1,150
Cost of Sales		Gizmo Costs	$350	
		Gadget Costs	200	
	Total Cost of Sales			$550

By breaking out both the sales and the cost of sales into greater detail, the P&L now shows that the business had $750 in Gizmo sales that cost them $350. The business more than doubled its money on the sale of Gizmos.

However, the business didn't do as well with its sale of Gadgets. The Gadgets it bought for $200, it sold for $400, only doubling its money.

What can a business owner do with this information? Perhaps she'll want to increase the price of Gadgets so she makes the same money on them as she does on Gizmos. Or perhaps she'll want to reduce the price of her Gizmos to sell even more at the same profit ratio as her Gadgets. Perhaps she'll decide to stop selling Gadgets and concentrate solely on Gizmos. There are many different scenarios she can consider, but only if the information is available.

In addition to breaking out the different product lines on the P&L, we can also insert additional line items that will help the business owner manage her business. One helpful one is Gross Profit. Gross Profit is calculated by subtracting the total cost of sales from the total sales. The Gross Profit for this period is $600 ($1,150 minus $550).

Let's enter the Gross Profit onto the P&L:
Under the words **Total Cost of Sales**, write **Gross Profit.**
To the right and directly below the $550 that has a line drawn under it for Total Cost of Sales, write $600.

Here is where we accountants can use our advanced arithmetic skills and calculate the Gross Profit Margin.

The Gross Profit Margin is Gross Profit displayed as a percent of Total Sales. It is calculated by dividing Gross Profit by Total Sales. In this case, the Gross Profit Margin is 52%. Write that next to the $600.

Your P&L should now look something like this:

PROFIT AND LOSS STATEMENT

Sales	Gizmo Sales	$750		
	Gadget Sales	400		
Total Sales			$1,150	
Cost of Sales	Gizmo Costs	$350		
	Gadget Costs	200		
Total Cost of Sales			$550	
Gross Profit			$600	52%

Of course, our business owner didn't make $600 in profit for this period. That is just the amount of the Gross Profit. We still need to deduct any other expenses she incurred. Let's add them to the P&L now:

Near the left edge of the page, aligned under the words **Cost of Sales** and just below the words **Gross Profit**, write **Expenses.**

To the right of the word ***Expenses*** and aligned under the words ***Gadget Costs***, write ***Rent.***

To the right of the word ***Rent*** and aligned below the $200 with the line under it for Gadget Costs, write $400.

Under the word ***Rent***, write ***Utilities.***

To the right of the word ***Utilities*** and under the $400 for Rent, write 0.

Under the word ***Utilities***, write ***Telephone.***

To the right of the word ***Telephone*** and under the 0 for Utilities, write another 0 and draw a line under it.

Your P&L should now look something like this:

PROFIT AND LOSS STATEMENT

Sales		Gizmo Sales	$750		
		Gadget Sales	400		
	Total Sales			$1,150	
Cost of Sales		Gizmo Costs	$350		
		Gadget Costs	200		
	Total Cost of Sales			$550	
	Gross Profit			$600	52%
Expenses		Rent	$400		
		Utilities	0		
		Telephone	0		

The list of possible expenses can go on and on for pages. They can include Wages, Payroll Taxes, Legal Fees, Accounting Fees, Office Supplies, Insurance, etc. You get the idea. In our example, they would all be zero during this period, except for Rent.

Let's also enter a total of all the expenses:

Aligned under the words ***Gross Profit*** and just below the word ***Telephone***, write ***Total Expenses.***

All the way to the right of the words *Total Expenses* and aligned under the $600 for Gross Profit, write $400 with a line under it.

We are now ready to calculate and enter the infamous *bottom line*, known in accounting as Net Profit. Net profit is Gross Profit minus Expenses.

Aligned under the word *Expenses* and just below the words *Total Expenses*, write *Net Profit.*

All the way to the right of the words *Net Profit* and aligned under the $400 with the line under it for Total Expenses, write $200 and draw two lines under it.

We can calculate the Net Profit Margin by dividing Net Profit by Total Sales. In this case, the Net Profit Margin is 17%. Write that number next to the $200.

Your completed Profit and Loss Statement should look something like this:

PROFIT AND LOSS STATEMENT

Sales	Gizmo Sales	$750		
	Gadget Sales	400		
Total Sales			$1,150	
Cost of Sales	Gizmo Costs	$350		
	Gadget Costs	200		
Total Cost of Sales			$550	
Gross Profit			$600	52%
Expenses	Rent	$400		
	Utilities	0		
	Telephone	0		
Total Expenses			$400	
Net Profit			$200	17%

There you have it, a separate Profit and Loss Statement that goes with the Balance Sheet.

Please note, the Net Profit on the Profit and Loss Statement *must* equal the total of the Profits or (Losses) on the Balance Sheet, otherwise your financial statements are not in balance with each other and would therefore be inaccurate.

By now, you should be feeling comfortable with the basics of accounting. As accountants, we look at all three parts of each financial transaction, and then we enter each one into the financial statements. Of course, we use accounting programs that make the reporting far easier than using a pencil and paper, but the *basics* are the same.

I hope you found this exercise helpful. I have a few more topics that might also improve your understanding of the basics of accounting.

Keep your Balance Sheet and your Profit and Loss Statement handy. I'm going to have you reference them in the next section.

DEBITS & CREDITS - DEFINED

I believe the words *Debit* and *Credit* are two of the most confusing words ever invented. When I was studying for my bachelor's degree in accounting, I was told this story:

> There once was a senior partner in a CPA firm whose office was in the basement of the building. No one else worked in the basement, but whenever anyone in the firm had an accounting question, they would always take it to the senior partner. Each time, the scene played out the same way.
>
> They would knock on his door and wait for his raspy voice to say, "Come."
>
> The door would creak open, and the senior partner would be sitting at his ancient desk, a green visor covering his eyes. He would look up and wait for their question.
>
> Once asked, the senior partner would always look up and to the left, as if the answer was somehow in the dark corner of the ceiling. A confused look would wash over his face, and he would then open his top left-hand drawer, look inside, and nod.
>
> Closing the drawer, he would answer whatever question had been asked. He was never wrong.
>
> When the senior partner died, the other members of the firm gathered outside his office, each one desperately wanting to know what secret of accounting knowledge lay hidden inside the old man's top left-hand drawer.
>
> They filed into the musty office and crowded behind the desk so they could all see. The new senior partner pulled open the drawer to reveal one small slip of paper. Printed on it, in neat block letters, was:
>
> *Debits are on the left*
> *Credits are on the right*

The point of the story is that the words *Debit* and *Credit* confuse everybody, including this senior partner. Their meanings are arbitrary and illogical. They can be used as adjectives, nouns, or verbs. And the trickiest thing about defining the words *Debit* and *Credit* is that you have to use the words *Debit* and *Credit* to define *Debit* and *Credit*.

It's an endless loop designed to give you a headache.

Please pull out your piece of paper with the Balance Sheet you made earlier. You're going to need it if you want to have any chance of understanding what I'm about to explain.

Debit and Credit Accounts on the Balance Sheet

On the left side of the paper, you listed Assets. Asset accounts are called debit accounts. Here we are using *debit* **as an adjective** to describe what kind of an account Assets are.

But what does it mean? Nothing, really. It's arbitrary. Don't try to make sense of it, just memorize it:

Debits are on the left

The other thing you must memorize is that the accounts on the right side of the balance sheet, the Liability and Equity accounts, are all called credit accounts:

Credits are on the right

Now that you have memorized that the accounts on the left side of the balance sheet are debit accounts and the accounts on the right side of the balance sheet are credit accounts, then I can use that information to explain to you what the words *Debit* and *Credit* mean.

> **As a noun**: a Debit increases the balance of a debit account or decreases the balance of a credit account, and a Credit increases the balance of a credit account or decreases the balance of a debit account.

Clear as mud, right? Do you remember the transaction we used earlier where the business owner received a loan from the bank and deposited it into her business checking

Understand Accounting

account? How did we enter that transaction into the balance sheet? We increased the balance in the checking account (where the money went) and increased the balance of the bank loan account (where the money came from).

In accounting jargon, we entered a ***debit*** for $900 in the Checking account and we entered a ***credit*** for $900 in the Bank Loan account.

A debit of $900 in a debit account (Checking is an asset which is on the left) increases the balance by $900. A credit of $900 in a credit account (Bank Loan is a liability which is on the right) increases the balance by $900.

Please don't ask me why accountants talk like this. After all these years, it's still a mystery to me.

> **As a verb**: to Debit an account is to increase the balance of a debit account or to decrease the balance of a credit account, and to Credit an account is to increase the balance of a credit account or to decrease the balance of a debit account.
>
> In other words, as verbs, they mean to take the action of entering a debit or a credit in the books.

Yes, I know. Your brain hurts. I'm sorry. There's a rumor these words were invented thousands of years ago by the very first accountant in history. His name was Satan.

Debit and Credit Accounts on the Profit and Loss Statement

Look at your Balance Sheet again. Notice that the Profits (or Losses) of the business are part of the equity section of the Balance Sheet. The equity section is on the right, under Liabilities. So, anything that increases the Profits of a business is a credit account and anything that decreases the Profits of a business is a debit account.

Now look at your Profit and Loss Statement.

What increases Profits? All income accounts. Therefore, they are *Credit* accounts.

What decreases Profits? All Cost of Sales and Expense accounts. Therefore, they are all *Debit* accounts.

Remember the transaction where the business owner paid her rent? How did we enter it in the balance sheet? We decreased the Net Profit by increasing Rent expense (where the money went) and we decreased the balance of the Checking account (where the money came from).

In accounting jargon, we entered a *debit* for $400 in the Rent expense account and we entered a *credit* for $400 in the Checking account. A debit of $400 in a debit account (Rent decreases Net Profit) increases the balance by $400. A credit of $400 in a debit account (Checking is an asset which is on the left) decreases the balance by $400.

By now, you're probably getting the idea why I teach accounting basics without using these two words.

Every Transaction has at least One Debit and One Credit

Because money comes *from* at least one place and goes *to* at least one place, every transaction entered into your books has at least two parts. Where the money comes from is always a credit, and where it goes to is always a debit.

Here are the transactions you entered earlier:
1. from Owner Contribution (credit) to Checking (debit)
2. from Bank Loan (credit) to Checking (debit)
3. from Credit Card (credit) to Furniture & Equip (debit)
4. from Accounts Payable (credit) to Inventory (debit)
5. from Sales (credit) and Accounts Payable (credit) to Accounts Receivable (debit)

5-Part 2. from Inventory (credit) to Cost of Sales (debit)
6. from Checking (credit) to Rent Expense (debit)

If you feel the need to review these definitions over and over again, you are not alone…

ACCRUAL VS. CASH

These two words have to do with the basis on which accounting is done. The basis means the timing of when financial transactions are recognized in the accounting reports (after all, we wouldn't want to have only one way to time the recognition of financial transactions).

For example, let's say a business receives a phone bill on June 4th. The bill is dated May 31st, and it is due on June 30th. Unfortunately, the business forgets to pay it until July 2nd. The expense could be entered as a May expense (when the phone expense happened), or it could be entered as a July expense (when the bill was paid). The timing of when the expense is recognized is dictated by the basis the business uses.

Accounting reports can be prepared on an *Accrual* basis or they can be prepared on a *Cash* basis.

Accrual Basis

In Accrual accounting, we recognize income when it is earned and expenses when they happened.

In the above example of the phone bill, we would recognize the Telephone Expense in May because that is the month in which the expense happened, regardless of when the bill was received or paid.

In our earlier example of the neighbor buying gizmos and gadgets out of the business owner's garage, we would recognize the Sale and Cost of Sales on the day of the sale, not when the customer eventually paid.

The reason for recognizing transactions on an accrual basis is to match the income generated during a period with the expenses that happened to produce that income. By matching the income with the expenses, we can accurately state whether or not the business made any money.

For the vast majority of businesses, preparing their reports on an accrual basis is the only way to accurately reflect the financial activity of their business.

Cash Basis

In Cash accounting, we recognize income when it is received and expenses when they are paid.

In the above example of the phone bill, we would recognize the Telephone Expense in July because that is the month in which the bill was paid, regardless of when the expense happened.

In our earlier example of the neighbor buying gizmos and gadgets out of the business owner's garage, we would recognize the Sale and Cost of Sales on the day the customer paid, not when the sale took place.

There are two primary reasons for preparing reports on a cash basis:
1. It is easier to do. The accountant only has to track the money coming and going from the bank and credit card accounts. No bills. No receivables.
2. It can postpone the payment of income taxes. If a business ends a year with a lot of receivables, they won't have to pay the taxes on those sales until after they receive the payments from their customers.

For most businesses the simple Cash basis will not provide them with an accurate reflection of their financial activity. And that can lead to poor business decisions.

How can a business owner know if she is making any money if her accountant doesn't match her income with the expenses that happened to produce that income? Most business owners can't. And if a business owner doesn't know if she's making any money, it's going to be hard for her to stay in business for very long.

Businesses that are primarily cash based, however, can use a Cash basis and still get relatively accurate financial reports. An example would be a coffee shop. Customers don't buy their coffee on terms, they pay at the register. And most of the vendors will expect immediate payment (because it's a coffee shop and may not be around next month). Therefore, cash based reports could be accurate enough.

Tax Basis

Just to confuse people a little more, we have this one more basis that is also used by accountants. This is how tax returns are reported.

The IRS allows most businesses to keep their books on an Accrual basis and still file their taxes on a Cash basis (of course the IRS makes exceptions, and they require some businesses to file their tax returns on an accrual basis).

Most tax preparers can easily convert Accrual based financial reports into Cash based tax returns with little problem. Some popular accounting programs, like QuickBooks, allow you to run the financial reports on either an accrual basis or a cash basis.

The rules for filing tax returns, like what has to be counted as income and what can be counted as expenses, may differ from both a strictly Accrual basis and a strictly Cash basis. And they can vary between federal returns and state returns. Therefore, tax returns are commonly referred to as being prepared on a Tax basis.

A business is not required to keep their books on a Tax basis, but they should maintain a schedule of the differences between the internal books (whether kept on an Accrual basis or a Cash basis) and their tax returns.

2 OUT OF 3 AIN'T BAD

I have found that business owners typically want their accounting systems to be all three of these things:

1. **Accurate** – as previously harped upon, financial reports are useless if they are not reasonably accurate.
2. **Timely** – the sooner a business owner can find out how the business is doing, the better chance she has to fix what isn't working (or do more of what is working).
3. **Inexpensive** – accounting doesn't generate any income, so business owners want to spend as little on it as possible.

Unfortunately, they only get to pick two of these three things. Any accounting system that is accurate and timely is not going to be inexpensive. If it's timely and inexpensive, it won't be accurate. And if it's accurate and inexpensive, then it won't be timely.

Of the three wants, inexpensive is the most important for the bottom line, but being accurate is critical to having any value at all. Timely is always desired, but seldom achieved.

Trade-offs are available, however.

As we discussed on page one of this book, financial reports don't have to be accurate down to the penny. Attempting to be that accurate would require waiting for every possible piece of information to arrive before preparing the financial reports. In some industries, that could take months.

Most of the time, it's better to estimate the transactions that are known to have happened, but the paperwork hasn't arrived. And if some of those transactions are estimated to the nearest $100, then the rest of the transactions don't need to be any closer than $100 either. I once had a client ask me to book an estimated expense of 75 cents, and this was after we had just booked other expenses estimated to the nearest $1,000. It was a waste of time.

The other trade-off is that the financial reports don't have to be immediate.

The cost of trying to achieve real-time accounting is staggering. A more realistic (and affordable) expectation is three weeks. By the 21st of the month, the financial statements for the previous month should be done. That allows three full weeks to gather all the information, enter all the transactions, estimate and enter anything missing that is known to have happened, reconcile the asset and liability accounts, and review the equity accounts and the profit and loss statement to ensure the reports are reasonably accurate.

If a business owner manages their expectations, they can receive relatively inexpensive financial reports that accurately reflect the financial activity of their business just three weeks after the end of each month.

And those reports can provide them with the information they need to make better business decisions.

Contact Information

I hope you have found this information helpful. If you have any questions, please email me at:

Tim@ShortridgeBusinessServices.com

Acknowledgements

This book would not have been possible without the support and assistance of my wife, and best friend, Corky Shortridge. She also happens to be my editor, proof-reader, and best critic. Thank you, thank you, thank you.

Other Books by
Tim Shortridge

Available on Amazon.com

Non-fiction

DON'T COOK FISH IN THE COMPANY MICROWAVE: How to Advance Your Career and Improve Your Life – by Tim Shortridge
(Tim Shortridge, 2015)

Do you look forward to going to work? Or do you go somewhere you don't want to go, to do things you don't want to do, with people you don't want to be around? If work isn't enjoyable, then this book can help.

Learn five simple steps to doing well and feeling good at work. Also included are 335 secrets and tips to help you advance your career (and which might help improve your life).

If your career is going great, but you're worried about how your children are doing at work, then this book would be a perfect gift for them. If your employees are not performing up to your standards, you should make this book required reading.

I have stumbled in my career so many times that it's embarrassing. Each time, it cost me dearly, either in time, money, or both. Mostly both. I wrote this book for my children because I didn't want them to duplicate the career mistakes I've made. I am now making it available to your children (and your parents' children) in hopes that it helps them, too.

NO PLACE TO RUN – As told by David Gilbert, written by Tim Shortridge and Michael D. Frounfelter (Vallentine Mitchell, 2002)

David and Sophie Goetzel moved from Germany to Warsaw, Poland in 1937 to escape the rising Nazi anti-Semitism at home. When the Germans invaded two years later, David vowed to keep his loved ones alive.

With dogged determination, the help of people he befriended along the way, and luck, he guided his wife and two-year-old daughter through the siege of Warsaw, imprisonment by the Gestapo, confinement in the Warsaw ghetto, going into hiding on the Aryan side of the city, eventual internment in Bergen-Belsen, and a terrifying train ride that led to liberation in 1945.

David, his wife, and his daughter all survived.

Michael Frounfelter and I wrote this true story about my friend David Gilbert in the style of a suspense / thriller. We've been told it reads as if John Grisham had written ***The Diary of Anne Frank****, but with a happy ending.*

Fiction

OUT OF PLUMB: A Quirky Collection of Humorous Short Stories and Poems – by Tim Shortridge (Tim Shortridge, 2015)

Need a quick laugh? This humorous collection of quirkiness will have you chuckling in no time.

SEALING FATE – a novel by Tim Shortridge
(Tim Shortridge, 2015)

There's an arsonist on the loose in San Diego County igniting wild fires in the dry, overgrown canyons whenever the Santa Ana winds blow. Doctor Vanessa Tornen lives with her mother and daughter in a house that overlooks one of those canyons.

When she accepts a position at a women's center, Doctor Tornen thinks she may have finally found the job, and perhaps even the man, of her dreams. Then a group of pro-life fanatics decides to shut down the center by intimidating their employees and their families.

Vanessa's entire world could come crashing down around her, if it doesn't go up in flames first.

Printed in the USA
CPSIA information can be obtained
at www.ICGtesting.com
LVHW041006220224
772549LV00017B/64